ıre

John B. Hilling
with drawings by Chris Jones-Jenkins

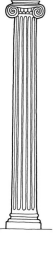

Introduction

Early Medieval

Romanesque

Early Gothic

Late Gothic

Tudor

Classical Renaissance

Buildings are an essential part of our heritage. They help us to understand how the people who used them lived, worked and worshipped. Whether they were raised speedily, in a quick constructional venture, or whether they were adapted, altered and added to over a long period of time, buildings tell us much about the social and artistic circumstances in which they were erected. In a sense, all buildings are historic and reflect the spirit and culture of their age.

We can also tell a lot about the buildings themselves by the way in which they were constructed, the materials that were used, and the styles of architecture that were employed. Constructional methods and architectural styles have changed over the centuries. By examining and understanding these, it is possible to assign an approximate date to a building, and to place it within its historic context.

In general terms, much of the architecture we see in Wales is derived from styles evolved elsewhere, particularly in England. But we should remember that historically much English architecture was, in turn, derived from styles first used on the Continent. In each case, the main difference between the local building and its source of inspiration is often a matter of degree. Buildings also vary in the way that they relate to topography, climate and social conditions.

The aim of this little book is to guide the reader in the recognition of the wide variety of buildings to be seen in the Welsh landscape and townscape. It also seeks to point out the main characteristics of construction and architectural style as they have been applied to Welsh buildings. Photographs and specially commissioned drawings are used to illustrate the text and to draw attention to key features.

The book also fulfils the function of a pocket guide to the architecture of Wales, from the early medieval period to the present day. It is divided into twenty-two short sections, each of which deals with a particular period or type of building. At the end of the book there is a list of important buildings and a map of their locations. Most of these, apart from churches and chapels, are in the care of Cadw, the National Trust, or local authorities and are open to the public. Those marked with an asterisk * are not open to the public but much of the important detail can be readily seen from outside.

Baroque

Rural Vernacular

Early Industrial

Historicism

Nonconformist Chapels

Arts and Crafts

Early Medieval

Early Christian

Remains of buildings erected in Wales between the departure of the Romans, late in the fourth century, and the arrival of the Normans, at the end of the eleventh century, are scanty in the extreme.

With the collapse of Roman authority came a revival of power centres based on easily defended sites. Sometimes, ancient hillforts, such as Dinas Emrys in Snowdonia, were reoccupied. Occasionally new sites were used. Thus the fort constructed during the fifth to seventh centuries on a craggy hilltop at Dinas Powys, near Cardiff, appears not to have had any earlier history.

In mid-Wales, a fortified crannog (artificial island) was built during the late ninth century at Llangorse Lake. The crannog was probably the site of the king of Brycheiniog's *llys* (court) and was constructed of sandstone on brushwood and timber, retained by vertical piles. The buildings have long since disappeared but were probably constructed of wood.

Llangorse: Impression of the crannog.

The memorial stones of princes and nobles have often survived better than their buildings. About 450 memorials remain from the early medieval period, mostly concentrated in south-west Wales. Many of these are connected with the early Christian church and range from crudely inscribed stones to elaborately sculpted and decorated pillar-crosses.

Silian: Ninth- or tenth-century decorated stone.

An important unifying feature during much of the period was the early Christian church. Celtic 'monasteries', comprising a number of small buildings enclosed by, or incorporated within, a curvilinear *llan* wall, were established in many coastal parts of Wales. Traces of such pre-Norman monastic settlements have survived on isolated islands at Ynys Seiriol (off Anglesey) in the north, and Burry Holms (Gower) in the south. Elsewhere, only the enduring decorated stone crosses give any physical hint of the importance of these ancient sites.

Nevern: Late tenth- or early eleventh-century high cross.

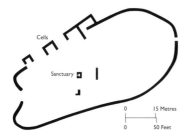

Puffin Island: Plan of early Christian monastic site.

Timber buildings have disappeared virtually without trace save for postholes which have been discovered during archaeological excavations. Monastic stone structures may well have been based on corbelled vaults similar to those found in early Irish oratories and later used as part of a continuing tradition in well-head buildings.

Carew: Eleventh-century high cross.

Brecon: Maen-du well with its corbelled stone roof.

Romanesque

Anglo-Norman Castles

In the late eleventh century, the Normans quickly overran the southern and the northern coastal lowlands of Wales, together with the Severn and Usk valleys. But after the initial thrusts, the Norman onslaught was brought to a halt and most of Wales remained in native hands. In the conquered areas the Norman lords erected castles to consolidate their hold.

Chepstow Castle: Great tower, 1067–1115.

Chepstow, one of the earliest stone castles in Britain, was built to guard the crossing of the Wye. The great tower, a large rectangular keep, was erected above the sheer cliffs overlooking the river. Windows were relegated to the secure, river side; so too was access with the exception of a large ceremonial doorway at the east end of the building.

Most of the early castles were constructed from earth and timber. The commonest type, known as a motte and bailey, comprised a large courtyard (bailey) — protected by a ditch and earthen rampart — and an artificial mound of earth (motte) surmounted by a wooden tower (keep). The tower acted as a lookout as well as the residence of the lord. The courtyard accommodated various service buildings.

Wiston Castle: An impression of the motte and bailey.

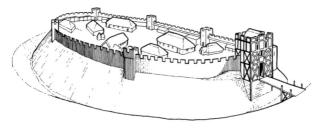

Kidwelly Castle: Impression of the ringwork.

A ringwork castle was a simpler type and may represent an earlier form of Norman fortification, or its form could have reflected topographical considerations. Ringwork enclosures were often raised above the surrounding ground level. They were generally defended by a deep moat and entered through a tall timber gatehouse.

Cardiff Castle: Shell keep.

When conditions permitted, many of the early castles were rebuilt in stone. Cardiff is a good example of a motte-and-bailey castle (constructed about 1081 within the remains of a Roman fort) where the original timber keep was replaced in the early twelfth century by a splendid stone shell keep. The fine gatehouse tower was added in the thirteenth century. The austere stone walls of Anglo-Norman castles are generally featureless apart from occasional arrowloops and flat, pilaster-like buttresses. Windows were generally small and round headed, and used sparingly. The main entrance, on the other hand, could be quite flamboyant as in the geometrically decorated doorway at Chepstow and the boldly detailed example at Newcastle, Bridgend.

Chepstow: Great tower doorway.

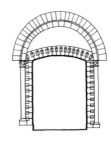

Newcastle, Bridgend: Curtain wall doorway.

Romanesque

Religious

When the Normans arrived in Wales they brought the Romanesque style with them. Architecturally, their most important type of building was the church. At first, most churches were stocky in appearance and relatively plain in design with simple, aisleless naves and chancels.

Walls of Romanesque churches are thick with shallow, flat buttresses and few openings. Herringbone masonry, similar to earlier Saxon construction, occurs sometimes in the south-east where most Romanesque buildings are located. Windows are round headed and tend to be narrow. Occasionally they are linked together or flanked by blind arcades.

Margam Abbey: West front, about 1170–80.

St Davids Cathedral: Nave, about 1180–1200.

Doorways are usually enclosed in semicircular arches. In later buildings doorways are often very decorative with tiers of receding arches ('orders'), each embellished with mouldings. Romanesque interiors are very heavy in appearance; openings seem to have been cut out of solid masonry. Columns are massive, usually square or cylindrical, occasionally octagonal or compound. Capitals at the tops of columns tend to be either square or round and have a cushion, scalloped, or, later, trumpet form. The heaviness was sometimes relieved by painted decoration in the form of ashlar joints and bell-like flowers as at Ewenny Priory.

Everywhere the semicircular shape is apparent: in doorways, windows, arches of the aisle arcades of larger churches and in barrel-vaulted ceilings (as at Ewenny Priory) where these were constructed in masonry. St Mary's, Chepstow,

Llandaff Cathedral: South doorway, about 1180–1200.

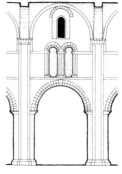

St Mary's Priory Church, Chepstow: Nave arcade (restored).

is on the site of the earliest Norman church (about 1072) in Wales. The present nave belongs to an early twelfth-century rebuilding.

Initially, stone barrel-vaulted ceilings were like semicircular tunnels extending along the length of the covered area. Rib vaulting developed from barrel vaulting as a means of reducing weight. But at first,

Penmon Priory: About 1140–70, with additions about 1220–40.

because arches were semicircular, it could only be used for covering square areas.

Towers were usually centrally placed — at the crossing — and were plain. In some churches in the north and west there is a distinctly Celtic flavour, both in the simplicity of structure — as in the pyramidal tops of some Anglesey towers — and the naturalistic, curvilinear decoration, as at Penmon Priory.

MOULDINGS

Romanesque is often characterized by rich decoration, notably mouldings in the form of bold geometric designs. Scandinavian influence is seen in the beakhead type of moulding and in the carved tympanum at Penmon Priory.

	Billet
	Chevron
	Cable
	Beakhead
	Nailhead

Early Gothic

Castles of the Marcher Lords

By the beginning of the thirteenth century, Anglo-Norman Marcher lords dominated the southern coastal strip and the Usk and Wye valleys, as well as exercising spasmodic overlordship of areas further inland. The latter areas were constantly under threat from Welsh princes. In order to maintain control many castles of the March had to be rebuilt.

Tretower Castle.

The craggy remains at Tretower illustrate this process. Initially, a motte-and-bailey castle was erected (near the Usk). In the mid-twelfth century this was replaced by an angular, stone shell keep. During the early thirteenth century, an imposing circular tower was erected within the earlier shell keep.

The inspiration for many round keep towers in Wales appears to have been the majestic donjon at Pembroke, which was built by William Marshal soon after 1200. Other Marcher lords in the south-east also erected round keeps to strengthen their castles. Round keeps were superior to rectangular keeps because they gave better all round fields of fire and had no corners that could be broken by battering rams.

Pembroke Castle: Keep, about 1200–05.

The entrance, accessible by wooden steps, was usually on the first floor; upper floors were reached by stone spiral stairs. In times of war the keep tower would have been crowned by a circular fighting platform or hourd.

Skenfrith Castle: Keep (restored).

The tops of walls were generally battlemented, or crenellated. The solid projections, known as merlons, often incorporated arrowloops.

The largest and most spectacular of all Marcher castles is Caerphilly, begun by Gilbert de Clare in 1268. It was surrounded by an artificial lake and equipped

Medieval crenellation.

with an almost impregnable system of defences, including five twin-towered gateways and an elaborate defence platform above a water barrage.

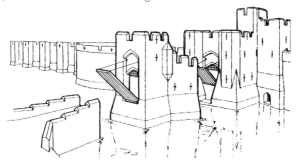

Caerphilly Castle: The main gate (restored).

THIRTEENTH-CENTURY ARROWLOOPS

The design of arrowloops, or loopholes, varied considerably. They were usually narrow vertical slots, splayed on the inside to give archers room to shoot.

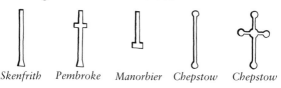

Skenfrith   Pembroke   Manorbier   Chepstow   Chepstow

Early Gothic
Castles of the Welsh Princes

Nearly forty earthwork and stone castles are known to have been built by the princes of Deheubarth, Gwynedd, Morgannwg and Powys. All of the Welsh stone castles that are now visible date from the thirteenth century, though there is evidence for earlier stone castles.

Most of the Welsh castles were located away from the sea, often on rocky sites, which dictated their irregular plans. Consequently, it was sometimes difficult to construct curtain walls in such a way that allowed a good field of fire from towers. Often the castles were defended by rock-cut ditches, but rarely had strong gatehouses.

Dolwyddelan Castle was built, probably by Llywelyn ab Iorwerth (Llywelyn the Great) between 1210 and 1240, to replace an earlier castle and has a rectangular keep. Rectangular keeps were also built at Castell y Bere, Dinas Brân and — as late as 1273 — by Llywelyn ap Gruffudd at Dolforwyn.

Map of native Welsh stone castles.

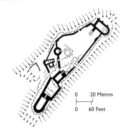

Plan of Castell y Bere.

Dolwyddelan Castle: Rectangular keep, 1210–40.

Round keeps were built at a number of castles both in the south and north. The round keeps of the Tywi valley, at Dinefwr (possibly built by Rhys Gryg, about 1220–33) and Dryslwyn, appear to have been influenced by Marcher castles in the south-east. In Snowdonia, Dolbadarn's dramatically sited round keep — probably built by Llywelyn ab Iorwerth about 1230–40 — was of sophisticated design with spiral stairs built within the thickness of the wall.

Dinefwr Castle: Circular keep (restored).

The apsidal, or D-shaped, keep at Ewloe, built about 1257 near the north-eastern border, was a compromise between the rectangular and round tower. The apsidal end overlooked the entrance and gave a better field of fire from the wallwalk than was possible from a rectangular tower.

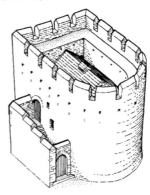

Ewloe Castle: D-shaped keep (restored).

Unusually, Criccieth was strongly defended by a massive gatehouse. The design was possibly influenced by English examples at Beeston and Montgomery. It was probably built by Llywelyn ab Iorwerth, about 1230–40, and comprises two apsidal towers on either side of the gate.

Criccieth Castle: Inner gatehouse, 1230–40.

Early Gothic

Edwardian Castles

In 1277 King Edward I unleashed a mighty force against the Welsh and followed this by building a chain of castles on the borders of Gwynedd, A further war followed, in 1282–83, during which Llywelyn ap Gruffudd, prince of Wales, was killed. With the collapse of Welsh resistance, Edward annexed Gwynedd and Deheubarth and began building another chain of castles along the coast.

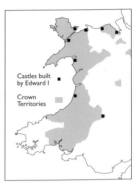

Wales in 1284.

New towns (bastides) were built alongside some of the castles. The purpose of these was to create centres of English influence within the heartland of Wales, as well as providing protection for officials and merchants. Each town was defended by walls and strong gateways and was laid out, wherever possible, to a gridiron plan.

Caernarfon: Plan of the castle and town.

The master mason in charge of building the castles was James of St George, a native of Savoy. Each castle was planned

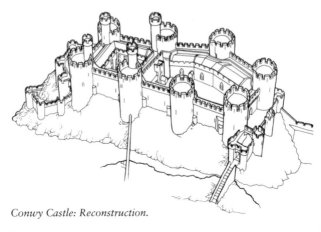

Conwy Castle: Reconstruction.

as an exceptionally strong fortress and incorporated the latest developments in military technology. Conwy, an outstanding achievement of medieval military architecture, stands on a rocky spur overlooking the river and is divided into two wards or baileys.

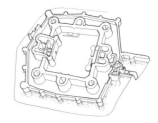

Beaumaris Castle: Begun 1295.

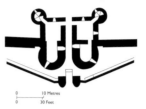

Harlech Castle: Plan of the gatehouse.

The inner ward at Conwy is defended by four great round towers, each surmounted by turrets. The adjoining outer ward is defended by similar towers, but without turrets.

Beaumaris is a classic example of the concentric plan, in which the inner ward is completely surrounded by an outer ward, like a box within a box. The symmetrical inner ward was designed with massive gatehouses and high curtain walls, from which arrows could be fired over the lower walls of the outer curtain.

Harlech Castle: Gatehouse.

Harlech is another example of the concentric plan, in this case built on a rocky hillside. The most striking feature is its enormous gatehouse with apsidal towers to the main gate and solid turrets overlooking the outer gate.

Caernarfon Castle: Eagle Tower.

Caernarfon was designed as a striking demonstration of imperial power as well as a mighty fortress. The horizontally banded stonework and angular towers were probably inspired by the Roman walls of Constantinople. The battlements of the Eagle Tower were decorated with stone figures, including an eagle.

Early Gothic

Religious

During the thirteenth century, church walls became thinner and lighter. This improvement was achieved by greater understanding of structural principles, better construction and larger windows.

Improvements, however, were only brought about gradually and over a long period. Often the hesitant transition between Romanesque and Gothic is indicated by a mixed use of features, as at Llanthony Priory where round-headed windows and pointed-arch recesses can be seen together on the western towers.

Llanthony Priory: West front, about 1200–20 (RCAHMW).

Gradually medieval builders realized that walls need only be very thick at the point where they are required to support the weight, or thrust, of arches. This led to the creation of buttresses, which were often stepped to provide greater depth and support.

Buttresses: Plain (left), stepped (right).

Windows: Triplet of lancet windows, Beddgelert (left); plate tracery, Bangor Cathedral (right).

The main characteristic of Gothic architecture is the use of pointed arches for windows, doorways and vaulting. Pointed-arch windows were at first tall, slim lancets. They were used either singly on side walls, or in groups on gable walls. Later, lancet windows were grouped together in clusters and the solid section between the pointed arches was pierced with smaller openings to create plate tracery.

The more important churches were enlarged by the addition of aisles. Aisles were separated from the nave by arcades of slender piers, linked by tall pointed arches. Circular or octagonal piers were often accompanied by delicate shafts, which increase the impression of verticality. Capitals to the piers and shafts were deeply cut and began to use naturalistic forms.

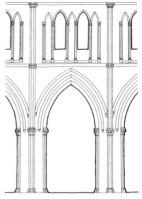

Llandaff Cathedral: Nave arcade, early thirteenth century.

Brecon Cathedral: Chancel vault (RCAHMW).

The pointed arch was developed on the Continent in answer to the need to cover rectangular areas with rib vaulting. The rib vaulting in the chancel of Brecon Cathedral was started in the late thirteenth century, but was not completed until 1862.

TOWERS

Towers became increasingly important symbolically as well as for lookouts. Apart from the usual pyramidal pitched roof there were regional variations, such as saddleback towers, mainly near the southern coast, and timber lantern-belfries, mostly in Powys and northern Monmouthshire. Spires were rarely built.

Lantern-belfry

Cross saddleback

Saddleback

Pyramidal

Gothic
Monasteries

Monastic communities, introduced from France by the Anglo-Normans, were an important part of Welsh medieval society. These highly organized monasteries differed from the earlier and simpler Celtic mother churches and were the result of far-reaching reforms that had taken place in the Continental church.

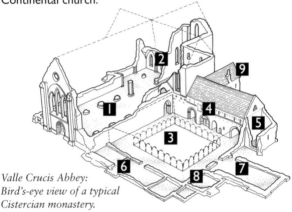

Valle Crucis Abbey:
Bird's-eye view of a typical
Cistercian monastery.

The earliest non-Celtic monasteries in Wales were sited in towns and belonged to the Benedictine order. The Cistercians, in contrast, placed great emphasis on austerity and sited their abbeys in isolated places away 'from the concourse of men', such as those at Strata Florida and Cwmhir.

Architecturally the communal concept of monasticism was expressed in a complex of buildings, the basic layout of which was common to most monasteries.

1. Church — nave, where lay brothers attended services.
2. Church — the rest of the church, including the transepts and presbytery, was reserved for the choir monks.
3. Cloister — an open court surrounded by covered passages.
4. East range, incorporating the chapter house, book room and monks' dormitory.
5. Latrine, linked to the monks' dormitory.
6. West range, incorporating cellars and lay brothers' dormitory.
7. Refectory or dining hall.
8. Kitchen, serving monks' and lay brothers' refectories.
9. Abbot's house.

Late Gothic

Religious

Advances in building techniques allowed fourteenth-century builders to experiment. Improvements in construction were matched with greater freedom in decoration and sculpture. The early part of this period is often known as Decorated due to the more ornamental design of windows.

Tintern Abbey: Decorated window in the church, about 1300.

Llandaff Cathedral: Ogee arch and reticulated tracery.

Clynnog: Perpendicular tracery.

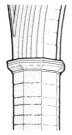

Brecon Cathedral: Octagonal pier with a moulded capital.

Deeper buttresses allowed thinner walls and this, together with the development of tracery, allowed windows to be wider. The solid plate tracery of the Early Gothic period evolved into light, geometric patterns. These were further developed into naturalistic curvilinear forms with sinuous ogee arches and net-like reticulated tracery. Doors too, became wider and some had graceful ogee arches.

Columns are sometimes octagonal or diamond shaped and often have fluting. Capitals to columns usually have simple, naturalistic foliage, or take plain moulded forms.

19

Ball-flower patterns were adopted for mouldings. Regularly spaced hook-shaped leaves, known as crockets, were used on sloping angles of canopies, spires and pinnacles.

Ball-flower ornament.

Towers were often added to churches. Occasionally, these incorporated steeply sided spires.

During the latter part of the fifteenth century and the early sixteenth century there was a boom in church building. This period is often known as Perpendicular. Vertical and horizontal lines predominate giving a feeling of increased height.

St Nicholas's, Grosmont: Fourteenth-century spire (RCAHMW).

Increasing wealth resulted in more complex layouts. Many existing churches were greatly extended and partly rebuilt and splendid new churches, particularly in the north, were erected.

Walls became skeletal with windows often taking up the space between buttresses. Windows became flatter and more angular; vertical mullions were carried right through to the arch.

New towers were usually bold and handsome, elaborately ornamented with pinnacles and openwork parapets.

In the south, many church roofs were constructed with arch-braced rafters and the whole ceiling panelled over to form a barrel or wagon vault. In contrast, open truss roofs strengthened by tie beams and windbraces, often decorated with cusps, are common in the north. A popular form of rebuilding in the north-east was the addition of a wide aisle — equal in width, length and height to the body of the church — thus creating a so-called double-nave church.

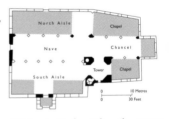

St Mary's, Tenby: Fifteenth-century extensions shown as shaded areas.

St Giles's, Wrexham: Tower.

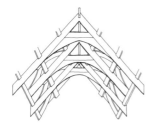

Roof with open trusses and windbraces.

Roof with panelled wagon ceiling.

Hammerbeam roofs with fine, panelled ceilings, often with carved bosses at junctions, are found in some of the larger churches of the north-east and elsewhere. At St Davids Cathedral the bosses of the timber-panelled ceiling were developed into decorative hanging pendants.

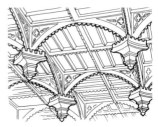

St Davids Cathedral: Panelled ceiling.

Elaborate stone vaulting was used comparatively rarely in Welsh churches. Expensive fan vaulting, in which the ribs radiate like a fan, was reserved for special situations such as the well chamber of the remarkable St Winifred's Chapel, Holywell.

Intricately carved rood screens and lofts were important features of many churches. Some excellent examples survived the hands of later iconoclasts in a few isolated places, such as Llananno, Llanfilo, Llanwnnog and Partrishow in Powys, and Betws Newydd in Monmouthshire. Those in the Severn Valley are bold and rich; those in the Black Mountains tend to be more restrained and delicate.

Partrishow: Rood screen and loft in the church of Merthyr Issui.

Late Gothic

Secular

With the demise of independent Wales at the end of the thirteenth century, the need for military fortifications declined and the castle gradually gave way to the manor house. In the more settled conditions that followed there was a growth in trade and improved rural prosperity.

An early type of manor house was the hall-house. In its commonest form this comprised three units. There was a ground-floor hall (open to the roof and heated by an open fire) in the centre, with service rooms at one end, and private rooms at the other. An ornate spere-truss sometimes marked the screens passage between the hall and the service rooms.

In some cases, as at Tretower, a castle might be abandoned altogether for a new house nearby. Here, in

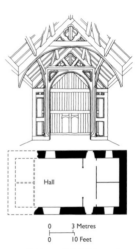

Penarth Fawr: Mid-fifteenth-century hall and plan.

the fifteenth century, a wing containing the hall with a fireplace was set alongside a suite of lodgings. The further addition of a gatehouse and wallwalks to form a protective courtyard reflect less settled conditions in the late fifteenth century.

Tretower Court: Fifteenth-century hall.

Tretower Court: Plan, about 1460–80.

St Davids Bishop's Palace: Wheel window.

St Davids Bishop's Palace: Parapet arcade.

The wealthiest landowners built extravagantly. Bishop Gower, (1328–47) for example, erected splendid palaces at St Davids, Swansea and Lamphey. The main rooms were at first-floor level, above vaulted undercrofts, typical of upper-class houses in the south-west. Each palace was surmounted by decorative, arcaded parapets and the great hall at St Davids was lit by a fine wheel window.

The most ambitious work of the latter part of the period was Raglan Castle. It combined a courtyard style with a military strongpoint. The detached and hexagonal great tower (1435–45), surrounded by a moat, was designed to withstand gunfire. The courtyard buildings were approached by an impressive gatehouse, defended by French-inspired machicolations.

Raglan Castle: Restored great gatehouse, about 1460.

Few multi-storey, fortified tower-houses were built in Wales. However, Llancaiach Fawr, in the Glamorgan uplands, seems to have links with both the tower-house and first-floor hall traditions. It is remarkable for the number of its mural stairs — useful as alternative escape routes — suggesting that even in the sixteenth century defence could still be an important aspect of design.

Llancaiach Fawr: Early sixteenth century.

Tudor

The 1536–43 Acts of Union, linking Wales permanently with England, may conveniently be taken as the beginning of the post-medieval period. After the contemporaneous Dissolution of the monasteries (1536–40), very few new churches were built; from the sixteenth to the eighteenth centuries the main type of building was domestic in character.

Tudor architecture was essentially a transitional style and can be seen as either the final phase of Gothic — with its emphasis on large windows and verticality — or the beginning of Renaissance ideals and formal planning. The E-shaped plan, with projecting wings and a centre porch, became fashionable for large houses. It allowed a symmetrical front elevation irrespective of the internal layout of rooms.

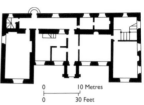

St Fagans: E-shaped plan, 1580.

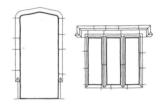

Tudor doorway and window.

Doorway heads became flattened, four-centred arches. Pointed windows almost disappeared, to be replaced by smaller rectangular, mullioned openings, except where large bay windows or projecting first-floor oriels were designed for architectural emphasis.

Increasing wealth provided opportunities for extensive rebuilding in the latest fashion by the nouveaux riches. At Carew Castle, for instance, Sir John Perrot added a

Carew Castle: Perrot's wing, 1588 (Colin Palmer).

Powis Castle: Long gallery, 1592.

magnificent new wing with giant windows and semicircular bays. There was also a piped water supply to the kitchen, although sanitation generally was still in its infancy.

Inside Tudor houses, there was a greater emphasis on comfort and privacy than had been possible hitherto. Flat ceilings replaced open roofs, and decorated plaster and wooden panelling were used extensively in the main rooms. Fireplaces were incorporated in as many rooms as possible, often resulting in a profusion of chimneys externally. Chimney pieces themselves were sometimes elaborately decorated.

Plas Mawr, Conwy: Decorated fireplace, 1580.

The appearance of buildings was increasingly influenced by those who had benefited from new opportunities for travel. For example, Sir Richard Clough — who had business interests in the Netherlands — incorporated Dutch-style crow-stepped gables on his own house, Plas Clough. It was such a successful feature that crow-stepped gables soon became used on many houses in the north, including Plas Mawr in Conwy.

Plas Mawr: Crow-stepped gable.

Classical Renaissance

The Renaissance, which had started life in fifteenth-century Italy as a revival of the classical culture of Greece and Rome, eventually arrived in Wales. Despite a few initial attempts at the beginning of the seventeenth century, diffusion of Renaissance ideas was slow to spread.

Architecturally, the Renaissance meant ordered and regular design derived from ancient building styles based on classical columns, together with pediments and other motifs associated with them. There were three Greek orders of columns, plus Roman modifications of these.

The hesitant introduction of Renaissance ideas can be clearly seen at Old Beaupre. Here, a late sixteenth-century extension included an outer gatehouse (1586) with a Tudor doorway enriched with pilasters and panelling in debased classical form. Fourteen years later, an extraordinary inner porch was added. This included three tiers of boldly coupled columns in each of the three orders.

Old Beaupre: Inner porch, 1600 (RCAHMW).

Important elements of Renaissance architecture were elevations designed to preconceived concepts and compact planning. Both of these appear in the design of Plas Teg (1610), a four-square building, which also included military-looking corner towers.

Great Castle House in Monmouth, although a townhouse and therefore even more compact, has a formal front obviously meant to impress visitors. Erddig was built on a much larger scale than either Plas Teg or Great

GREEK ORDERS

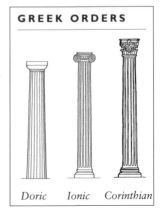

Doric   *Ionic*   *Corinthian*

Castle House. In this case the very simplicity of the symmetrical main front, with its long rows of sash windows, emphasizes its grandeur. Like the more elaborate Tredegar House (1670) in the south, Erddig was surrounded by formal gardens, which complemented the regular lines of the house.

Great Castle House, Monmouth: 1673.

Erddig: 1684.

Interiors were planned on ordered principles with large entrance halls and prominent staircases. The main rooms were often placed on the first floor and were plastered or finished in wood panelling. Ceilings might also be panelled or decorated with high-relief plasterwork.

Chirk Castle: Long gallery, 1678 (RCAHMW).

A few major landowners erected chapels of ease on their estates, but new parish churches were built only infrequently. The harmonious, neat furnishings of Gwydir Uchaf chapel echo contemporary house interiors.

Gwydir Uchaf chapel: 1673.

Baroque to Picturesque

The eighteenth century was a period of great activity and increased prosperity as a result of improved agricultural methods and new industrial development. While many new mansions appeared in the countryside, this was also an important period for urban building, particularly in regional centres such as Brecon, Carmarthen, Denbigh, Monmouth, Swansea and Welshpool.

At the beginning of the century there was an excursion into baroque, a style based on classical architecture but developed in an original and 'plastic' way. Giant columns and pilasters, emphatic curves and projections, and broken pediments were typical features.

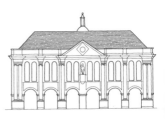

Shire Hall, Monmouth: 1724.

After the brief baroque interlude, architects returned to a more dignified style based on designs of the sixteenth-century Italian Andrea Palladio. Rules of proportion and standards of taste were firmly established

Llandaff Court: 1744–51.

and gradually these percolated down to ordinary builders. Porches and triangular-shaped pediments were frequently used, but buildings remained rather austere.

Throughout the eighteenth century there was an emerging current of Romanticism, and it was not long before this lighter spirit appeared in architecture. The elegant orangery at Margam, with its floral central parapet and rusticated windows, was one development.

Another development was neo-Gothic, which had resulted from an increasing interest in medievalism. The Gothic character of eighteenth-century buildings was only skin-deep, however, and when allied to the Picturesque movement, as at Hafod (now demolished), it produced some bizarre, almost oriental, results.

Margam: The orangery, 1787.

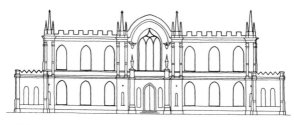

Hafod: 1786.

The Picturesque movement arose out of an interest in 'natural' landscapes. In an attempt to imitate nature, and persuade nature to imitate art, landscape gardeners contrived sinuous lakes, grottoes and follies. The follies were meant to be seen from a distance and were often in the form of neo-Gothic 'ruins' such as the sham castle at Clytha.

Towards the end of the century, John Nash set up his office in Carmarthen and while there developed his Romantic classical style. He designed a number of small country houses, such as Llanerchaeron, which were typically built to a square plan with rooms arranged around a central staircase. The handsome appearance of these houses was based on their simple, well-mannered elevations.

Clytha Castle: 1790.

Llanerchaeron: 1794 (RCAHMW).

Rural Vernacular

Vernacular buildings are utilitarian structures that have been constructed in traditional ways using locally found materials. They were not conceived by professional designers and are generally unpretentious in character.

The appearance of a building depends, to a considerable extent, on the materials used. These materials vary according to what was available in the different areas of Wales. The map shows the regional distribution of timber, undressed stone, and clay as the main materials for walls. Brick was also used in some border areas from the late sixteenth century.

Distribution of half-timbered (A), stone (B) and clay (C) buildings.

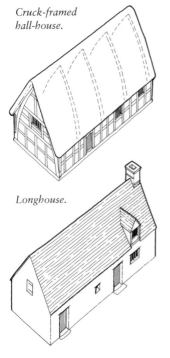

Cruck-framed hall-house.

Longhouse.

The cruck-framed, single-storey, hall-house appears to have been the dominant type of dwelling over large areas — except the south-west — prior to the late Tudor period. It was heated by an open fire in the hall. Construction was based on rows of trusses, each formed out of two curved crucks and set up as inverted 'V's.

The longhouse was once common in upland areas. It comprised a long, rectangular building housing both family and cattle under the same roof, but divided at the centre by a common access passage serving both parts. The passage was also used as a feeding walk for the cow-house.

By the late sixteenth century, storeyed houses had begun to supersede hall-houses. The form of the post-medieval house varied from region to region and was largely determined by the position of its main fireplace. In the north-west the dominant type of storeyed house had the fireplace on the end wall(s), resulting in gable chimneys.

Stone house with gable chimneys.

In the eastern borderlands and mid-Wales, the usual position of fireplaces (often back-to-back) was in the centre of the house. The late seventeenth-century house shown is from Powys and is half-timbered, with an entrance lobby backing on to the fireplace.

Half-timbered house with central chimney.

A third type of house had the fireplace on one of the longer, main walls. This was common in the south-west (where it was often accompanied by massive chimneys), and along the southern coastal areas.

Stone house with lateral chimney.

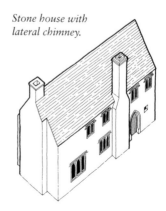

In the fifteenth century, nearly all domestic buildings, apart from great houses, belonged to the vernacular tradition; by the nineteenth century only the meanest cottages fell within this group.

31

Early Industrial

Industry of one kind or another had existed in Wales since prehistoric times. These industries were, however, generally of a small-scale nature. It was not until the eighteenth century that major, innovative changes began to take place — particularly in the iron and coal industries.

Many early industrial buildings, such as the barn-like blast furnace at Dyfi, were vernacular in character. The Dyfi furnace used charcoal to smelt iron ore. Materials were taken to the upper floor and tipped into a shaft-like furnace from a high-level charging platform. A waterwheel, on one side of the building, was used to drive bellows to create the blast.

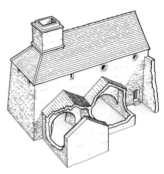

Dyfi Furnace: 1755.

By the end of the eighteenth century, iron making in the south and north-east had been transformed; coal had replaced charcoal as a fuel and steam was used instead of water-powered bellows to provide blast. Iron furnaces became much larger and were built in groups, their tapering external shells echoing their internal shape.

Neath Abbey Ironworks: Blast furnace, 1793.

Equally distinctive features of most nineteenth-century ironworks were the towers needed to lift materials from the works yard to the charging level. The tower at Blaenavon was of the water-balance type and consisted of a lift that could be raised and lowered by filling or emptying tanks of water.

Blaenavon Ironworks: Balance tower, 1839.

Llanberis: Slate workshop, 1870.

Although industrial buildings were basically functional structures, they were often designed to impress. A good example of this conscious formality is to be seen at the slate quarry workshops, Llanberis. In north-western Wales, slate quarrying was the major industry. With

Ynysfach: Engine house, 1830s.

improvements in transport, slate began to be used extensively for roofing in all parts of Wales.

Large engine houses were required in a number of industries to provide power. Nineteenth-century engine houses were often impressively designed and included regularly positioned windows. Colliery winding houses had tall, round-headed windows and sometimes resembled Nonconformist chapels.

Most eighteenth- and nineteenth-century housing was built by private contractors. Occasionally, dwellings were built by industrial owners as 'company houses'. These were usually built to house key workers and although just as uniform as other terraced houses, they were often of better quality and slightly larger in size.

Most industrial housing was unplanned. At Tredegar, a complete new town with a geometric layout centred on a circular market place was created between the ironworks and the ironmaster's park during the years 1810 and 1818, making it the first consciously planned industrial town in Britain.

Blaenavon Ironworks: Stack Square, 1789–92.

Historicism

Castellated Mansions

The background to nineteenth-century architecture is the so-called 'battle of the styles' during which various earlier architectural styles were revived. In domestic buildings, both revived Gothic and revived classical styles were used and argued over; hence the term 'battle'.

Cyfarthfa Castle: 1825.

Initially, Gothic was the favourite mode for the 'castles' of the newly rich entrepreneurs and industrialists. Hawarden — a handsome eighteenth-century classical house — was thoroughly transformed into a castellated mansion; Gwrych was built as a new 'fortress' complete with curtain walls and eighteen towers; Cyfarthfa was designed to overawe the workers who laboured in virtually medieval conditions for its owner.

Penrhyn Castle: 1827–40.

More architecturally convincing than any of the above shams, however, was the Norman-style Penrhyn Castle, built for the owner of a slate-rich estate. It took thirteen years to complete and its monumental 'keep' was closely based on the twelfth-century keep tower of Hedingham Castle in Essex.

For sheer ostentatious extravagance, Castell Coch and Cardiff Castle were easily the most remarkable resurrections of the nineteenth century. Castell Coch had been a ruin and the restoration there was a serious attempt to reconstruct, in French Gothic style, a castle as it might originally have appeared.

Castell Coch: Section showing old (solid) and new (hatched), 1871–89.

Cardiff Castle: Clock tower, 1874.

Both Castell Coch and Cardiff Castle were greatly altered and rebuilt to designs by William Burges (d.1881). The restoration of the latter was more extensive and included, amongst its additions, a Romantic clock tower piled high with exotically decorated rooms.

Various other styles were tried including 'Tudorbethan'. Perhaps the most curious reconstruction was Gregynog Hall, which was transformed about 1870 into an extensive, many-gabled mansion, faced in concrete with imitation half-timbering.

Gregynog Hall: 1870.

Pure 'classical' architecture was too restrained for the grand tastes of most Victorian builders, and comparatively few great houses were built in this style. Clytha in Monmouthshire, and Glynllifon and Rug in the north are the main examples. The more seductive French Renaissance was tried in a few instances, notably for the entrance front at Kinmel Park. The garden front at Kinmel has Dutch overtones, as too does the delightful gate lodge.

Kinmel Park: Gate lodge, 1870.

Historicism

Public Buildings

Many of the most interesting works of nineteenth-century architecture were public and educational buildings, erected in the more prosperous county towns and in growing centres of importance. As with the other buildings of the period they reflected the historic styles of the past.

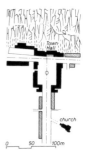

Tremadog: Market hall and square, 1800–11(left); plan (right).

During the early part of the century most types of building could be clearly identified with one or other of the historic styles. Tremadog, a tiny 'new' town built at the beginning of the century (1800–11), symbolized this relationship of type and style. The church there was Gothic, the Nonconformist chapel was Greek, and the elegant market-cum-town hall — built at the end of an attractive Renaissance-style piazza — was Italianate.

Swansea: Royal Institution of South Wales, 1841.

Some of the most successful public buildings belonged to the Greek Revival. This was an academically pure style, which had been started in England in the mid-eighteenth century and was then popularized in France and Germany. The rather stately Royal Institution of South Wales in Swansea, with its Ionic portico, is a good example of the Greek Revival.

Another important Greek Revival building is the old Shirehall in Brecon. Here, the symmetrical entrance front reflects the axial planning of the interior. After the middle of the century, Greek influence gave way to a more ponderous, but still classical, Roman-inspired style.

Brecon: Shirehall, 1842.

The larger educational buildings were generally built in some form of Gothic or Tudor style. St David's College, Lampeter, was built in the form of a stuccoed

Lampeter: St David's College, 1827 (RCAHMW).

quadrangle with corner turrets reminiscent of a late medieval academy. Occasionally the Dutch-inspired Queen Anne style was also used.

The University College at Aberystwyth, on the other hand, actually started life as a hotel. It was converted into a college in 1872 but then, a few years later, was partly burnt down. Enough, however, remains of the southern and northern wings, along with the staircase tower, to appreciate the extraordinary neo-Gothic design of this architectural fantasy.

Aberystwyth: University College, 1885 (RCAHMW).

Historicism
Gothic Revival Churches

The architectural style used for most Anglican churches built in Wales during the nineteenth century was either Romanesque (semicircular arches) or Gothic (pointed arches). The earliest Gothic churches of the nineteenth century, such as Tremadog (1806) and Milford Haven (1808), tended to be plain and raw, as though their designers were unsure of the correct details.

In the fast growing industrial towns of the south, Romanesque was often adopted for the churches built by the iron companies. St David's Rhymney (1843), also in the south, is a rare example of a classical church. Romanesque was also the style sometimes used for 'economical' churches built in the 1830s and 1840s with the aid of parliamentary grants. The best of these is St Mary's in Cardiff's Butetown.

Cardiff: St Mary's, Butetown, 1843.

However, it was Gothic, in all its varieties, which remained the most popular style. John Prichard, the best-known Welsh architect of the nineteenth century, favoured early Gothic for his imaginative restoration (1843–67) of Llandaff Cathedral. The remaining cathedrals were all restored by Sir George Gilbert Scott (d. 1878), one of the better-known English architects working in Wales. Penpont — partly rebuilt and partly extended in Early Gothic — is a fine example of Scott's smaller church restorations.

Penpont: North elevation (above) and plan of church (below), 1865.

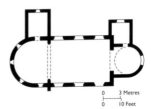

0 ___ 3 Metres
0 ___ 10 Feet

Decorated Gothic later became even more fashionable than early Gothic, and one of the most striking churches of the mid-nineteenth century, the so-called Marble Church at Bodelwyddan, is in this style. It was built in white limestone and is dominated by a tall, slim tower and a splendid spire. In similar style, but quite different in appearance, are St Mary's, Halkyn (1878), with its squat tower, and St German's, Cardiff (1884), with its lofty interior.

Bodelwyddan: St Margaret's, 1860.

A popular feature used in many late Victorian churches was constructive colouration. The most successful example of this form of decoration is at St Augustine's, Penarth. Here, yellow Bath Stone and pink sandstone were used for the columns and arches and red brickwork —— filled with black and white diaper-work — for the walls, producing a warm and colourful space. Another fine example of polychromatic decoration can be seen at St Catherine's, Baglan (1882), a cruciform church with tall spire and elaborate interior.

Penarth: St Augustine's, 1866.

Nonconformist Chapels

Nonconformist meeting houses first appeared in Wales as far back as the seventeenth century. The earliest chapel to have survived is Maes yr Onnen, 1696. During the eighteenth century, the Nonconformist movement gathered strength and new chapels — often converted farmyard barns like Maes yr Onnen — were established in many parts of Wales.

Maes yr Onnen, 1696.

The vast majority of chapels was built during the nineteenth century. The earliest were single storey and very simple in design. Typically, the main façade was on one of the long walls. Internally, the pulpit was placed at the centre of the long wall, symmetrically between two tall windows.

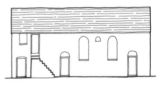

Beili Du, about 1820.

Often chapels were rebuilt once, twice, or even three times during the nineteenth century to accommodate growing congregations. Sometimes a first-floor gallery was added to provide

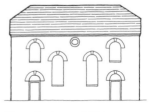

Llwynrhydowen, 1834.

Pontypridd: Tabernacle, 1861.

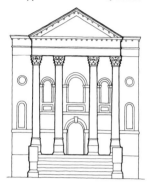

Carmarthen: English Baptist, 1872.

additional accommodation. The main façade was still a long wall; two separate entrances — one for men and the other for women and children — were retained.

In the fast-growing towns, space was at a premium, so chapels were sited at right angles to the road with the entrance at the pine end. Typically, a single entrance, tall, round-headed windows, and a circular central window were incorporated in the design to emphasize the importance of the gable elevation.

As more and more chapels were built or rebuilt they became larger and more elaborate. Most were built in a classical, rather than Gothic, style. Windows on the main elevation were normally round-headed and the triangular upper part of the gable gradually took the form of a classical pediment.

When funds allowed, full-blown classical features were used to emphasize the dignity and importance of the chapel. In the larger towns wealthier congregations were able to erect thoroughly classical buildings, complete with projecting porticoes and Corinthian columns.

During the latter part of the nineteenth century, the external designs of chapels became more decadent and mannerist, although interiors often became more elaborate and remarkable. Chapel building continued unabated until the First World War. One of the principal chapel architects of this period was Beddoe Rees (d. 1931). At Ebenezer he experimented with a neo-Renaissance design for a circular chapel.

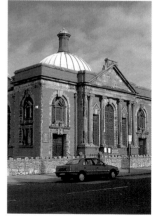

Llandudno: Ebenezer, 1909.

Arts and Crafts to Neo-classicism

Even before the twentieth century, the character and purpose of architecture was undergoing a reappraisal. The early years of the new century were, consequently, a period of both hopeful experimentation and wistful looking backwards.

The Arts and Crafts movement, which arose in the late nineteenth century, emphasized craftsmanship and traditional methods but rejected historicism and was thus a precursor of the modern movement. St Mark's church, Brithdir, was intended to look 'as though it had sprung out of the soil, instead of being planted on it'.

Brithdir: St Mark's, 1896 (RCAHMW).

Typical of the styleless vernacular, which the Arts and Crafts movement aimed to create, was the domestic architecture of C. F. A. Voysey (d. 1941). In the Cardiff example shown here, free planning and bold but clean-cut elevations endowed the house with a fresh simplicity and naturalness.

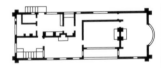

Cardiff: A house of 1903.

Caldey Island: Monastery, 1910–12 (RCAHMW).

Bangor: University College, 1911.

Another, transient, influence on non-traditional architecture was the attenuated and flowing lines of art nouveau. Both Arts and Crafts and art nouveau influences are apparent in the work of J. C. Carter. In the monastery at Caldey, Carter was also influenced by the German Romanesque style.

Indeed, historicism was not dead and traditional styles continued to be revived well into the twentieth century. Thus, the University College at Bangor was designed in the romantic spirit of the Gothic Revival — although with Jacobean detailing so that it looks, from a distance, more like a great medieval monastery than a modern educational institution.

In Cardiff's outstanding civic centre, all the buildings constructed before the Second World War were designed in some form of classical style. The design of each, however, was influenced by different sources. The symmetrical front of the National Museum & Gallery, for instance, was influenced by North American versions of classical Greece.

Cardiff: National Museum & Gallery, 1910–27.

During the years immediately before the Second World War, neo-classical architecture began to evolve in a different direction. This development was marked by a watering down of classical motifs, resulting in austere buildings with a superficial feel of modernism. This abstract neo-classicism is typified by the smooth, unemotional, but symmetrical lines of Swansea's Guildhall.

Swansea: Guildhall, 1934.

Early Modern

The essence of modernism is the rejection of historicism. One of the principal ingredients of modernism is functionalism. This design philosophy held that the functional aspects of a building were of paramount importance and should be reflected in its appearance.

Criccieth: Moranedd cafe, 1948.

Modern functionalist architecture, in the sense that 'form follows function', first appeared in Wales early in the twentieth century, prior to the First World War, with some unadorned concrete structures associated with coal mining, such as coal preparation plants and coking plants (all demolished). They were the precursors of what later came to be known as the 'international style'. Although the term was not coined until 1932, the first examples of the international style had appeared on the Continent soon after the First World War. The style was characterized by sleek lines and smooth geometrical forms, emphasized by flat roofs and large glazed areas.

Although generally rare in Wales, the international style was used appropriately for welfare buildings to suggest a vision of 'a brave new world'. An important example was the tuberculosis hospital at Sully, with its white-rendered walls, full-height windows and faceted façades. Many miners' pithead

Barry: Sully Hospital, 1932–36 (RCAHMW).

baths, such as those at Penallta Colliery (1938), Gelligaer, were also built in the style.

Concrete was one of the favourite materials of early functionalist architects as this allowed large spans to be covered and difficult forms, such as domes, to be constructed, as at the innovative Brynmawr rubber factory in 1947–51 (demolished). Reinforced concrete and steel frames were used to advantage in multi-storey tower blocks where similar floor slabs could be supported on comparatively thin columns.

Carmarthen: Trinity College hostel, 1965.

Aberdare: Llwydcoed Crematorium, 1970.

In practice, the principles of functionalism often proved difficult to apply in a pure way and, with the passing of doctrinaire ideas, a more flexible approach to modern architectural design began to take place. This can be seen, for instance, in a number of sensitively designed and laid-out schools built in Montgomeryshire (north Powys) during the 1950s. Gradually, designs began to reflect more expressionist or allusive attitudes. Exemplars of these tendencies are to be found in religious buildings and their counterparts, such as crematoria. Not surprisingly, they tried to evoke feelings of the highest order.

By the 1970s, more imaginative use of forms, materials and colour helped to give large public buildings a warmth and humanity that had sometimes been lacking in earlier functionalist examples.

Aberystwyth: University great hall and library, 1970–76.

Late Modern

During the last quarter of the twentieth century, the functionalist approach to building design has continued to develop in different ways. Apart from the so-called post-modernist style, which is basically concerned with decoration and symbolism, three concepts have emerged.

Llanarthne: Great glasshouse, 2000 (Nigel Young/Foster and Partners).

High-technology buildings are characterized by their use of advanced materials, highly organized structure, and sophisticated service equipment. They often reflect new trends, or, as in the glass dome of the great glasshouse at the National Botanic Gardens, take structural methods to extreme limits. In some high-technology designs the buildings have been virtually turned inside out to display both their structure and their services.

In contrast to high-technology designs, buildings employing 'green' technology use sustainable 'natural' materials and well-insulated walls instead of expensively produced components. The use of naturally found or grown materials, including grass

Newport: High-technology factory, 1982.

Narberth: Nant-y-Cwm Steiner Kindergarten, 1989 (RCAHMW).

Caernarfon: Plas Menai Outdoor Pursuits Centre, 1982 (Plas Menai).

roofs, together with the need to minimize energy requirements by recycling, help to give 'green' buildings their characteristic handmade appearance.

In the third and wider group the way that structures and services are used is less outwardly important than the way in which the building's functions, or image, are expressed. In both Plas Menai Outdoor Pursuits Centre and the headquarters of the Snowdonia National Park Authority, for instance, cascading, slate roofs and low profiles are intended to emphasize the traditional aspects of a large, modern building so that they can be more easily integrated into the landscape. At the Wales Millennium Centre the function of each part of the building is reflected in its external shape, while the building's 'Welsh' credentials are emphasized by the use of materials from different parts of the country and the incorporation (in enormous letters) of verses in Welsh and English.

Some buildings, such as that for the National Assembly for Wales (designed in 1998), display all three concepts. In this new building, vast areas of glass and slim structural supports emphasize both its use of high-technology methods and its democratic 'transparency', while the method of extracting air naturally from the circular debating chamber via a wind-tower lantern is evidence of its 'green' technology.

Cardiff: National Assembly for Wales, due to open in 2005.

Gazetteer and Map of Important Buildings

To help readers find the sites listed in the gazetteer, the nearest large town is noted together with the Ordnance Survey grid reference. A grid reference is also given to locate sites on the map.

EARLY MEDIEVAL: EARLY CHRISTIAN
1 **Burry Holms**, Swansea, **C7** (SS 400925).
2 **Carew Cross**, Pembroke, **B6** (SN 047037).
3 **Maen Achwyfan Cross**, Prestatyn, **E1** (SJ 129788).
4 **Nevern Cross**, Cardigan, **B5** (SN 083400).
5 **Llanbadarn Fawr Church**, Aberystwyth, **C4** (SN 599810).
6 **Llantwit Major Church**, Llantwit Major, **E7** (SS 966687).
7 **Penmon Priory**, Beaumaris, **D1** (SH 630807).
8 **Margam Stones Museum**, Port Talbot, **D7** (SS 801864).

ROMANESQUE: ANGLO-NORMAN CASTLES
9 **Cardiff**, **E7** (ST 181766).
10 **Chepstow**, **F7** (ST 533941).
11 **Coity**, Bridgend, **D7** (SS 923815).
12 **Kidwelly**, Llanelli, **C6** (SN 409071).
13 ***Monmouth**, **F6** (SO 507129).
14 **Newcastle**, Bridgend, **D7** (SS 902801).
15 **Ogmore**, Bridgend, **D7** (SS 882769).
16 **Wiston**, Haverfordwest, **B6** (SN 022181).

ROMANESQUE: RELIGIOUS
17 **Ewenny Priory**, Bridgend, **D7** (SS 912778).
18 **Llandaff Cathedral**, Cardiff, **E7** (ST 155781).
19 **Margam Abbey**, Port Talbot, **D7** (SS 802863).
20 **Penmon Priory**, Beaumaris, **D1** (SH 630807).
21 **St Davids Cathedral**, St Davids, **A6** (SM 751254).
22 **St Mary's**, Chepstow, **F7** (ST 535939).
23 **St Peter's**, Cogan, Penarth **E7** (ST 168705).
24 **St Woolos Cathedral**, Newport, **F7** (ST 309876).

EARLY GOTHIC: CASTLES OF THE MARCHER LORDS
25 **Caerphilly**, **E7** (ST 155870).
26 **Caldicot**, **F7** (ST 487885).
27 **Kidwelly**, Llanelli, **C6** (SN 409071).

28 **Laugharne**, Carmarthen, **C6** (SN 302107).
29 **Manorbier**, Pembroke, **B6** (SS 065978).
30 **Pembroke**, **B6** (SM 982016).
31 **Skenfrith**, Abergavenny, **F6** (SO 457202).
32 **Tretower**, Crickhowell, **E6** (SO 184212).

EARLY GOTHIC: CASTLES OF THE WELSH PRINCES
33 **Criccieth**, **C2** (SH 500377).
34 **Dinas Brân**, Llangollen, **E2** (SJ 223431).
35 **Dinefwr**, Llandeilo, **C6** (SN 612217).
36 **Dolbadarn**, Llanberis, **C2** (SH 586598).
37 **Dolwyddelan**, Betws-y-Coed, **D2** (SH 721523).
38 **Dryslwyn**, Llandeilo, **C6** (SN 555204).
39 **Ewloe**, Connah's Quay, **F1** (SJ 288675).
40 **Castell y Bere**, Tywyn, **D3** (SH 667085).

EARLY GOTHIC: EDWARDIAN CASTLES
41 **Aberystwyth**, **C4** (SN 579815).
42 **Beaumaris**, **C1** (SH 607762).
43 **Caernarfon**, **C1** (SH 477626).
44 **Conwy**, **D1** (SH 783774).
45 **Flint**, **E1** (SJ 274733).
46 **Harlech**, **C2** (SH 581312).
47 **Rhuddlan**, **E1** (SJ 024779).

EARLY GOTHIC: RELIGIOUS
48 **Bangor Cathedral**, Bangor, **C1** (SH 580720).
49 **Beddgelert**, **C2** (SH 590480).
50 **Brecon Cathedral**, Brecon, **E5** (SO 044289).
51 **Llanbadarn Fawr**, Aberystwyth, **C4** (SN 599810).
52 **Llanddew**, Brecon, **E5** (SO 054307).
53 **Llanthony Priory**, Abergavenny, **F6** (SO 289278).
54 **Llantwit Major**, **E7** (SS 966687).

GOTHIC: MONASTERIES
55 **Cwmhir Abbey**, Llandrindod Wells, **E4** (SO 005571).
56 **Neath Abbey**, Neath, **D6** (SS 737974).
57 **Strata Florida Abbey**, Aberystwyth, **D4** (SN 746657).